WHY DO I
DROOL?

BY HARRIET BRUNDLE

CRABTREE
PUBLISHING COMPANY
WWW.CRABTREEBOOKS.COM

Published in Canada
Crabtree Publishing
616 Welland Avenue
St. Catharines, ON
L2M 5V6

Published in the United States
Crabtree Publishing
PMB 59051
350 Fifth Ave, 59th Floor
New York, NY 10118

Published in 2019 by Crabtree Publishing Company

First Published by Book Life in 2018
Copyright © 2018 Book Life

Printed in the U.S.A./082018/CG20180601

Author: Harriet Brundle

Editors: Kirsty Holmes, Kathy Middleton

Design: Danielle Rippengill

Proofreader: Janine Deschenes

Prepress technician: Samara Parent

Print coordinator: Katharine Berti

All facts, statistics, web addresses and URLs in this book were verified as valid and accurate at time of writing. No responsibility for any changes to external websites or references can be accepted by either the author or publisher.

Photographs

All images are courtesy of Shutterstock.com, unless otherwise specified. With thanks to Getty Images, Thinkstock Photo and iStockphoto. Front Cover & 1 – Dmitry Natashin, Nadzin, Sudowoodo, Sunflowerr. Images used on every spread – Nadzin, TheFarAwayKingdom. 2 – svtdesign, vectorplus, anpannan. 4 – Iconic Bestiary. 5 – Makc, Iconic Bestiary. 6 – Iconic Bestiary. 7 – Le_Mon, lenjoyeverytime. 8 – LOVE YOU. 9 – MaryValery. 10 & 11 – Le_Mon, Iconic Bestiary. 12 – Iconic Bestiary, Maxim Cherednichenko, Sudowoodo. 13 – Iconic Bestiary. 14 – world of vector, Ign. 15 – Iconic Bestiary, Karolina Madej, VikiVector. 16 – Le_Mon, wissanustock, lenjoyeverytime. 17 – svtdesign, vectorplus, anpannan. 18 & 19 – Le_Mon. 20 – Meranda19. 21 – Pretty Vectors, Skokan Olena. 22 – Iconic Bestiary, Miuky. 23 – Ign, ArtMaster85, Artem Twin, George J.

Library and Archives Canada Cataloguing in Publication

Brundle, Harriet, author
        Why do I drool? / Harriet Brundle.

(Why do I?)
Includes index.
Issued in print and electronic formats.
ISBN 978-0-7787-5134-2 (hardcover).--
ISBN 978-0-7787-5147-2 (softcover).--
ISBN 978-1-4271-2171-4 (HTML)

        1. Mouth--Juvenile literature. 2. Human physiology--Juvenile literature.
I. Title.

QP146.B73 2018   j612.3'1   C2018-902396-1
                                                              C2018-902397-X

Library of Congress Cataloging-in-Publication Data

Names: Brundle, Harriet, author.
Title: Why do I drool? / Harriet Brundle.
Description: New York, New York : Crabtree Publishing Company, 2019. |
  Series: Why do I? | Includes index.
Identifiers: LCCN 2018021330 (print) | LCCN 2018021666 (ebook) |
  ISBN 9781427121714 (Electronic) |
  ISBN 9780778751342 (hardcover) |
  ISBN 9780778751472 (pbk.)
Subjects: LCSH: Saliva--Juvenile literature. | Salivary glands--Juvenile literature. |
  Drooling--Juvenile literature. | Human physiology--Juvenile literature.
Classification: LCC QP191 (ebook) | LCC QP191 .B78 2019 (print) |
  DDC 612.3/13--dc23
LC record available at https://lccn.loc.gov/2018021330

CONTENTS

Words that look like **this** can be found in the glossary on page 24.

Is Your mouth Watering?

Does your mouth water when you smell something tasty? That water is called saliva.

Think about your favorite food. Is your mouth starting to water?

Do you ever wake up with a wet pillow? Sometimes saliva leaks out when you are asleep. That is one way we drool. To drool is to leak saliva from our mouths.

Sometimes people can drool when they are awake, too.

Crunch and Slurp

You use your teeth to chew your food into smaller pieces. This makes it easier for your body to break down the food when it reaches your stomach.

Your mouth makes a lot of saliva when you chew your food. Saliva begins to break down the food even before you swallow it.

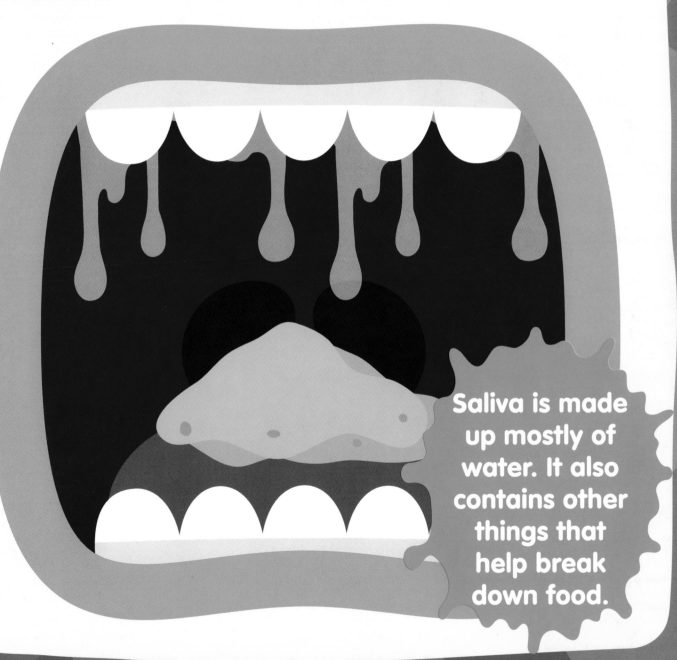

Saliva is made up mostly of water. It also contains other things that help break down food.

Busy Mouths

There are different body parts inside and around your mouth. They all help you digest, or break down, your food.

Teeth cut and crush your food.

The little bumps on your tongue are called taste buds. They tell your brain what food tastes like.

Body parts **called** glands make saliva.

Food travels down to your stomach through a long tube connected to **your** throat.

Your tongue moves the food around inside your mouth.

Saliva also helps to keep your mouth wet.

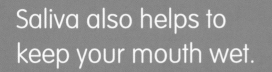

Imagine trying to talk or swallow with a very dry mouth. It would be almost impossible!

Chew and Swallow

STEP 1:

As soon as you take a bite of food, your saliva goes to work!

STEP 2:

Your glands send saliva into your mouth as you chomp down on food. The more you chomp, the more saliva is sent.

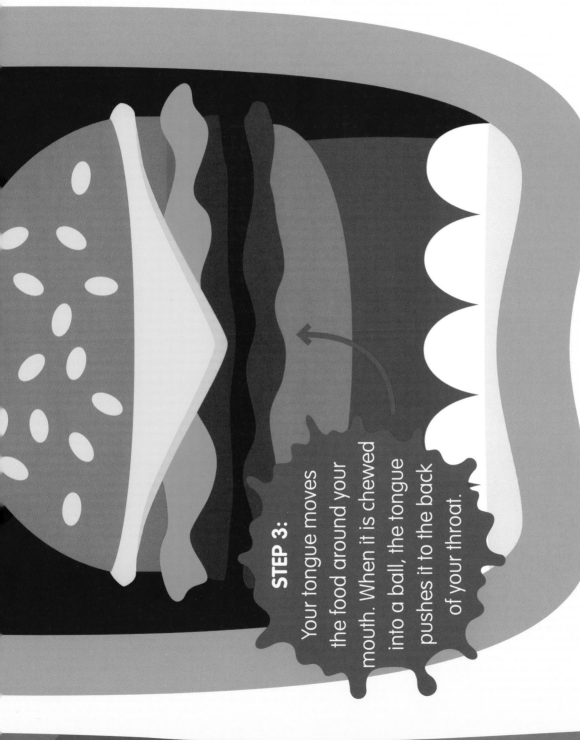

STEP 3:

Your tongue moves the food around your mouth. When it is chewed into a ball, the tongue pushes it to the back of your throat.

STEP 4:

Finally, you swallow. Saliva helps the ball of food slip down your throat easily.

11

Drool Drool

So why does your mouth water when you smell something delicious?

When you smell food, your brain thinks you are about to eat. It sends instructions to the glands to prepare your mouth for the meal by filling it with saliva!

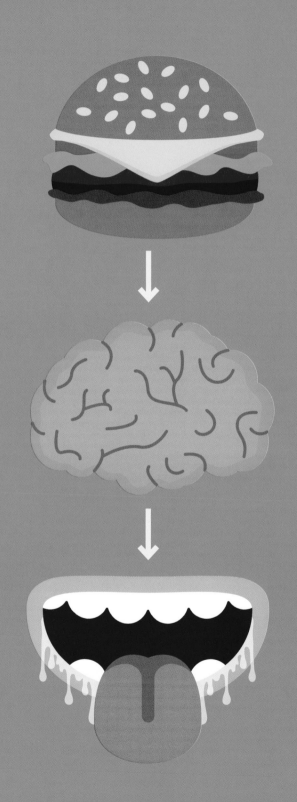

You swallow your saliva when you are awake. You don't swallow saliva when you are asleep. Saliva builds up in your mouth. It can sometimes leak out as drool.

Stick Your Tongue Out

Don't forget to brush your tongue when you brush your teeth. This helps keep it clean and gives you fresh breath!

Our tongues are covered in taste buds. Each person has thousands of taste buds on their tongue.

Your taste buds tell your brain what food tastes like. This is how you can tell if food tastes salty, sweet, sour, and bitter.

Some people love the bitter taste of lemons. Others love super-sweet ice cream!

Show Us Your Teeth

The mouth has different types of teeth. They all work together to bite and crunch food.

The flat teeth at the back are the biggest. They chew and grind food.

The teeth in the middle bite off chunks.

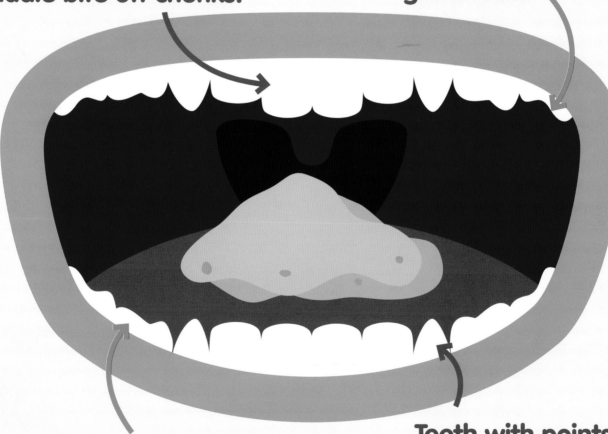

A flatter surface helps teeth crush food.

Teeth with points are used to rip and tear food.

Saliva, the Superhero!

Your teeth are protected by strong **enamel**. Saliva helps protect your teeth's enamel.

A coating of saliva on your teeth also helps fight off germs that cause cavities.

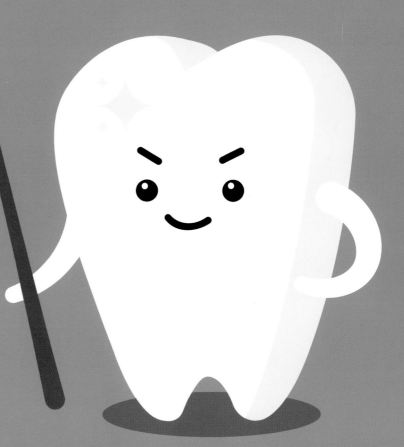

A Recipe for Saliva

Our saliva is made up of a special mix of different ingredients.

About **99 percent of your saliva is made of water.**

Saliva also contains things that help break down food in your mouth before you swallow it.

Saliva helps keep your **mouth** moist. **This helps you speak and swallow.**

The mouth makes 2 to 4 pints (1 to 2 L) of saliva each day.

Saliva works every day to help keep our mouths clean and healthy.

Saliva washes away bits of food that get stuck between your teeth.

Anything else you put in your mouth, such as toothpaste, can be found in your saliva.

Dust or dirt can also end up in your saliva!

Super Spit!

Did you know that saliva has several different superpowers?

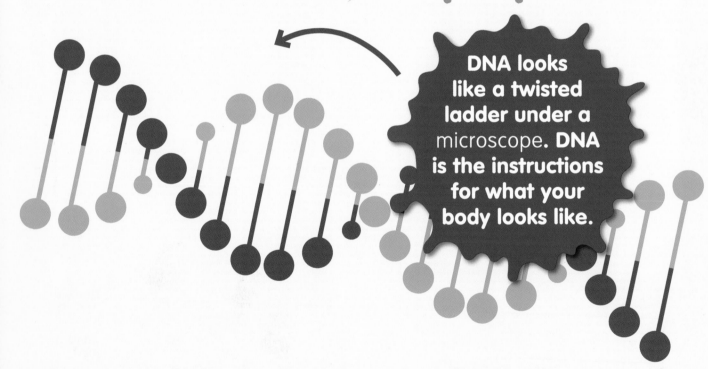

DNA looks like a twisted ladder under a microscope. **DNA is the instructions for what your body looks like.**

Information about your entire body can be found inside your mouth. Saliva contains all of your body's DNA information!

There is something called opiorphin in human saliva which acts like medicine to ease pain!

Vampire bat saliva can be lifesaving! Some people develop lumps, called clots, in their blood. These lumps can be dangerous because they can block the flow of blood to parts of the body. Luckily, vampire bat saliva has something in it we can use to stop blood from making lumps.

Drool Trivia

With the help of saliva, cuts in your mouth heal faster than cuts anywhere else on your body!

Each year, you produce enough saliva to fill two bathtubs!

Sometimes something hard like a stone can form inside the glands that produce saliva. They can also form inside other body parts.

The largest stone ever removed from a human body was 1 ½ inches (3 ¾ cm) long.

Brian Krause holds a record for spitting a cherry pit 93 ½ feet (28 ½ m).

You produce less saliva when you are feeling nervous or frightened. That makes your mouth feel pretty dry.

Glossary

cavities   Holes that develop in the teeth

enamel   A hard substance that acts as a protective coating for our teeth

glands   Parts of the body that produce substances, such as saliva and sweat

microscope   A tool that makes tiny objects appear bigger

moist   Damp or wet

throat   The body part that leads from the mouth and nose to the long tube that connects to the stomach

tongue   The body part in the mouth used for talking, tasting, and swallowing food

Index